LOTS AND LOTS OF COINS

Margarette S. Reid

illustrations by True Kelley

DUTTON CHILDREN'S BOOKS   An imprint of Penguin Group (USA) Inc.

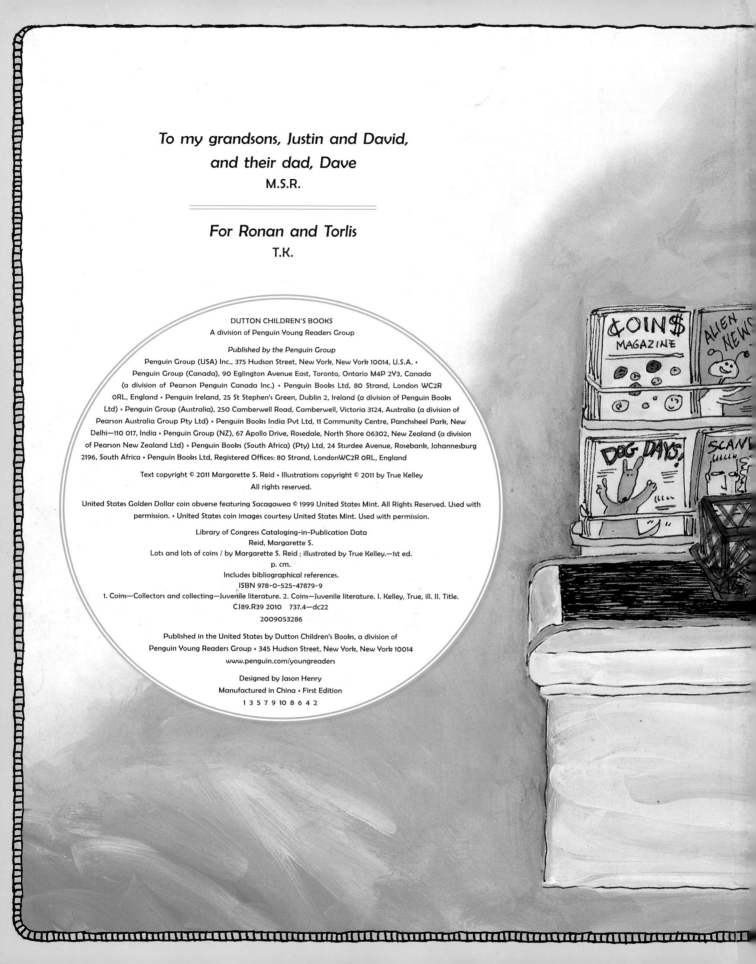

To my grandsons, Justin and David,
and their dad, Dave
M.S.R.

For Ronan and Torlis
T.K.

DUTTON CHILDREN'S BOOKS
A division of Penguin Young Readers Group

Published by the Penguin Group
Penguin Group (USA) Inc., 375 Hudson Street, New York, New York 10014, U.S.A. •
Penguin Group (Canada), 90 Eglington Avenue East, Toronto, Ontario M4P 2Y3, Canada
(a division of Pearson Penguin Canada Inc.) • Penguin Books Ltd, 80 Strand, London WC2R
0RL, England • Penguin Ireland, 25 St Stephen's Green, Dublin 2, Ireland (a division of Penguin Books
Ltd) • Penguin Group (Australia), 250 Camberwell Road, Camberwell, Victoria 3124, Australia (a division of
Pearson Australia Group Pty Ltd) • Penguin Books India Pvt Ltd, 11 Community Centre, Panchsheel Park, New
Delhi—110 017, India • Penguin Group (NZ), 67 Apollo Drive, Rosedale, North Shore 06302, New Zealand (a division
of Pearson New Zealand Ltd) • Penguin Books (South Africa) (Pty) Ltd, 24 Sturdee Avenue, Rosebank, Johannesburg
2196, South Africa • Penguin Books Ltd, Registered Offices: 80 Strand, LondonWC2R 0RL, England

Library of Congress Cataloging-in-Publication Data
Reid, Margarette S.
Lots and lots of coins / by Margarette S. Reid ; illustrated by True Kelley.—1st ed.
p. cm.
Includes bibliographical references.
ISBN 978-0-525-47879-9
1. Coins—Collectors and collecting—Juvenile literature. 2. Coins—Juvenile literature. I. Kelley, True, ill. II. Title.
CJ89.R39 2010   737.4—dc22
2009053286

Published in the United States by Dutton Children's Books, a division of
Penguin Young Readers Group • 345 Hudson Street, New York, New York 10014
www.penguin.com/youngreaders

Designed by Jason Henry
Manufactured in China • First Edition
1 3 5 7 9 10 8 6 4 2

My dad carries paper money in his wallet to buy things. When he spends paper money he usually gets change back. He does this a lot and so we have plenty of coins to look at together.

Are you a collector?

May I see the change?

DORIS

WARNER MARKET

Dad and I think coins are cool. He's a coin collector. I learn a lot about coins from him.

Dad says coins have been around for a long time—hundreds of years, even thousands of years. Once Dad made me laugh. He emptied a pocketful of beads and shells. That's what people used to use for money.

Here, you can keep the change.

Here, you can keep the change.

Shell it out, Dad! Ha ha.

Ha ha, very funny! I'm glad coins were invented.

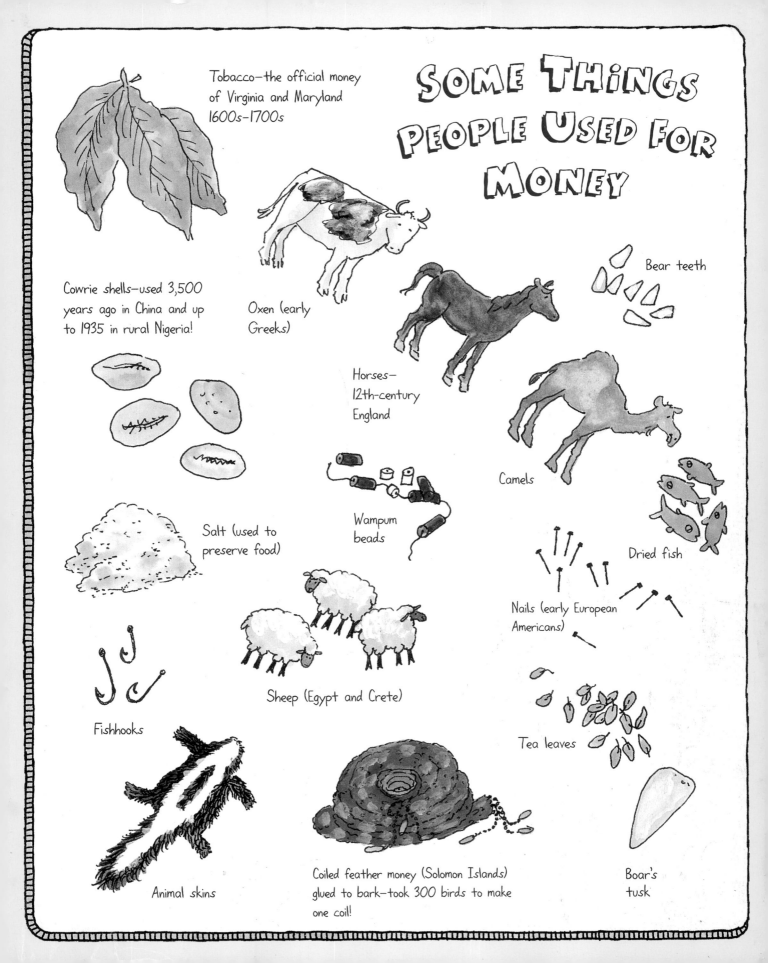

SOME THINGS PEOPLE USED FOR MONEY

Tobacco—the official money of Virginia and Maryland 1600s–1700s

Cowrie shells—used 3,500 years ago in China and up to 1935 in rural Nigeria!

Oxen (early Greeks)

Bear teeth

Horses—12th-century England

Camels

Salt (used to preserve food)

Wampum beads

Dried fish

Nails (early European Americans)

Fishhooks

Sheep (Egypt and Crete)

Tea leaves

Animal skins

Coiled feather money (Solomon Islands) glued to bark—took 300 birds to make one coil!

Boar's tusk

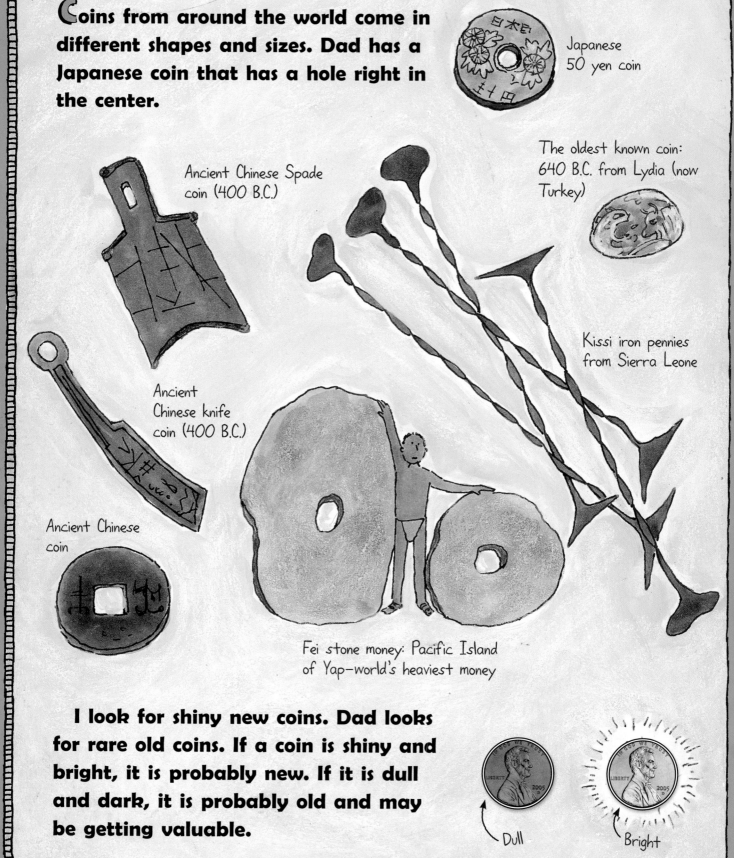

Coins from around the world come in different shapes and sizes. Dad has a Japanese coin that has a hole right in the center.

Japanese 50 yen coin

The oldest known coin: 640 B.C. from Lydia (now Turkey)

Ancient Chinese Spade coin (400 B.C.)

Kissi iron pennies from Sierra Leone

Ancient Chinese knife coin (400 B.C.)

Ancient Chinese coin

Fei stone money: Pacific Island of Yap—world's heaviest money

I look for shiny new coins. Dad looks for rare old coins. If a coin is shiny and bright, it is probably new. If it is dull and dark, it is probably old and may be getting valuable.

Dull

Bright

Dad doesn't spend the coins he collects. He fits those into a special folder to protect them. Printed on the folder is the year the coin was struck at the mint.

"That's its birthday," he says. I laugh. I think it is funny to say that coins have birthdays.

"**W**hat does 'struck at the mint' mean, Dad? I thought a mint was red-and-white-striped candy!"

Dad smiles. "The mint is where coins are made."

The first U.S. Mint facility in Philadelphia, 1792.

The U.S. Mint facility at Philadelphia, today. There are also United States Mint facilities in Denver, San Francisco, and West Point.

Look for the mint mark on a coin.
D=Denver, S=San Francisco, P=Philadelphia, W=West Point.

Plain, round metal disks are put in a powerful machine. It *strikes* two different pictures into the metal.

One side is called heads, and the other side is called tails.

Flipping a coin is one way to decide who gets the first turn.

.HEADS.

LIBERTY
IN GOD WE TRUST
1986

.TAILS.

UNITED STATES OF AMERICA
QUARTER DOLLAR

Heads, I win.

Tail!

Tails, I win! Heads, you Lose! Ha! Ha!

Dad says if a mistake is made at the mint, an odd coin may become a treasure to collectors.

A 1955 penny: double printed could be worth $12,000!

The three-legged 1937 buffalo nickel could be worth thousands!

Struck off-center: a coin is worth more with a readable date and mint mark.

This penny was clipped off at the mint.

A penny with a nickel printed on top.

Coins are different colors, depending on the metal used to make them.

Penny

COPPER

1974 Uncirculated Penny, made from Aluminum

ALUMINUM

1849 Liberty Head Dollar

GOLD

Dime

SILVER

600 B.C. Lydian coin

ELECTRUM

1684 Tin Farthing (British)

TIN

Electrum is a mix of gold and sliver.

After we finish checking for special coins, Dad puts the rest of the change in an old fishbowl. I call it my coin collection. I stir those coins and look through the glass at them, all mixed up.

When I look at my coins, it's fun to pretend I'm rich, but I've found out that it takes a whole lot of change to buy a soccer ball or a hamster at the pet store. You have to save up for the things you really want.

$3.95

$20.00

doesn't cost a mint

$250.00

ONLY $14.99

WHAT A DEAL!

$12.00

$4.99

$38.99

$175.00

Dad and I make a game of sorting coins by size. I close my eyes and pick a coin out of the fishbowl.

First, I find a penny. A penny is also called a cent.

The Abraham Lincoln penny was issued in 1909 to celebrate the 100th anniversary of his birth.

. THE PENNY .

· HEADS ·   · TAILS ·

The United States Mint produces over a thousand pennies a second.

The Lincoln Memorial, Washington, D.C.

It takes one hundred pennies to buy something that costs one dollar.

Look for the tiny letters VDB. They are the initials of the artist Victor David Brenner.

Next, I find a smaller, thinner coin. It's a dime. Ten dimes equal a dollar.

Equal is an important word. It means that different things have the same value.

President Franklin Roosevelt

. THE DIME .

· HEADS ·   · TAILS ·

The dime is the smallest coin we use today.

Olive and oak branches, flaming torch.

PIGGY BANK · FACTS ·

10¢ = 1 dime

THE DIME GAME

Place dimes in this pattern. Make the triangle point up (instead of down) by moving only three dimes.

A quarter is bigger. It takes four quarters to equal one dollar.

e pluribus unum means "one of many"
(many peoples = one nation)

President George Washington

. THE QUARTER .

· HEADS ·   · TAILS ·

George Washington did not want his face on a coin. He thought it would make him look like a king.

PIGGY BANK
· FACTS ·
25¢ = 1 quarter

I feel around for the biggest coin. It's called a half-dollar. It takes two half-dollars to equal a whole dollar.

50¢ 50¢

=

THE UNITED STATES OF AMERICA
ONE DOLLAR

The Presidential Seal

. THE HALF-DOLLAR .

LIBERTY
IN GOD WE TRUST
2005

· HEADS ·

UNITED STATES OF AMERICA
HALF DOLLAR

· TAILS ·

The Kennedy half-dollars were first released in 1964 and were over 90% silver.

President John F. Kennedy

The eagle faces the symbol of peace, olive branches. In his other claw are arrows, representing war.

PIGGY BANK
· FACTS ·

50¢ = 1 half-dollar

DESIGN YOUR OWN COIN!

LIBERTY
IN GOD WE TRUST
1969

Trace around a half-dollar and then draw your design.

AWESOMENESS BE COOL!

UNITED STATES OF AMERICA
100 DOLLARS

I like to make rubbings of coins. I tape the coin to the back side of the paper and rub the front side with a pencil.

I line the coins up in order of size.

Then I line them up in order of their value.

50¢

25¢

10¢

5¢

1¢

Sometimes a big coin is worth less than a small coin!

Dad says, "Coins are like a piece of history you can hold in your hand."

New nickels celebrated the anniversary of the purchase of the western lands.

President Thomas Jefferson sent Lewis and Clark to explore the West. One nickel shows how they traveled by keelboat.

Captain Lewis designed the boat that is shown on this coin himself! It was 55 feet long and could be rowed, sailed, towed from the riverbank, or poled like a raft.

WESTWARD JOURNEY
KEELBOAT NICKEL
· 2004 ·

Another shows the peace medal they gave to the Indian people they met.

WESTWARD JOURNEY
PEACE MEDAL
NICKEL
· 2004 ·

Another westward journey nickel has the words "O! The joy!" It tells how they felt when they saw the Pacific Ocean for the first time.

There are a lot of different presidents on coins. At school we learn about the ones who helped found our country.

James Madison

Thomas Jefferson

John Adams

George Washington

PRESIDENTIAL DOLLARS
· 2007–Present ·

In 2007, the U.S. mint began a new series of one-dollar coins. Each coin features a president, starting with George Washington. Four new coins are made each year.

"Hey," I tell Dad, "all those Founding Fathers had long hair." I put their coins in one pile.

braham Lincoln goes in a different pile. He wore a beard.

All my pennies have Abraham Lincoln's picture on the front, but they have different pictures on the back. The first Lincoln pennies have a picture of wheat sheaves on the back. Then came a different picture—the Lincoln Memorial. The newest change shows four different times in Lincoln's life.

I sort the pennies by the design on the back.

Was I the only president with a beard?

Some rare coins are worth a lot of money. Founding Father Benjamin Franklin's designs were used on the first penny authorized by the United States Congress. I wanted to see that penny, but Dad didn't have one. He said that penny is worth more than a thousand dollars now.

One thousand dollars! ($1,000!) That's one hundred thousand pennies! (100,000!)

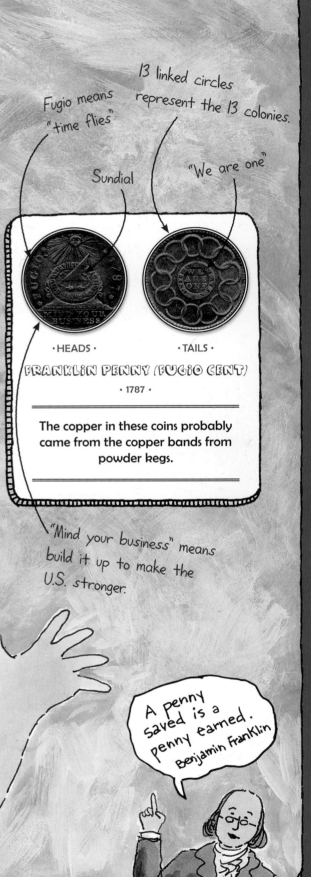

Fugio means "time flies"

13 linked circles represent the 13 colonies.

Sundial

"We are one"

· HEADS ·   · TAILS ·

FRANKLIN PENNY (FUGIO CENT)
· 1787 ·

The copper in these coins probably came from the copper bands from powder kegs.

"Mind your business" means build it up to make the U.S. stronger.

A penny saved is a penny earned. Benjamin Franklin

Sometimes Dad and I have so many coins that we take them to the bank to trade for paper money. We used to count out sets of coins and fill paper tubes with them, but now there are machines that do the counting for us.

I like to see all that money!

I'm glad coins keep changing. That's what makes them so much fun—especially when I collect them with my dad.

AUTHOR'S NOTE

A coin is a piece of history you can hold in your hand. It is exciting to find a lost coin. See a penny. Pick it up. All the day you'll have good luck! Look between the couch cushions and in the washing machine. Did you find a nickel? Does it have a buffalo on it? In 1913 James E. Fraser designed one of the most popular nickels ever minted. It featured an animal that was uniquely American although it no longer roamed the western prairies. James Fraser was acutely aware of this loss and honored both the buffalo and Native Americans with his beautiful design.

A new buffalo design appeared on a nickel in 2006. This time the buffalo faces to the right, not the left. Indeed the buffalo has returned to the lands it once roamed. If you go to your public library, you can become a history sleuth and discover many fun facts about coins. Librarians love to help kids find books on subjects in which they are interested.

A librarian helped the author find a wonderful picture book that tells the story of James E. Fraser and the 1913 buffalo nickel. It is *The Buffalo Nickel* by Taylor Morrison, Houghton Mifflin Company, Boston, Massachusetts, 2002.

She also helped me find these interesting books about coins: *The Coin Counting Book* by Rozanne Lanczak Williams, Charlesbridge Publishing, Watertown, MA, 2001 and *Follow the Money* by Loreen Leedy, Holiday House, Inc., New York, N.Y., 2002.

Every coin ever minted in our country is described in *A Guide Book of United States Coins* by R. S. Yeoman, edited by Kenneth Bressett. It is updated each year. There is also a U.S. Mint web site at http://www.usmint.gov/kids/index/cfm. Here you can find out great facts about coins and even take a tour of the mint!

Coins are a wonderful hobby to share with your family and friends. Be a coin collector. It's fun!

If you collect coins, you are a numismatist! (new-MIZ-mah-tist)

Dime Game Answer   Don't Peek!